FACT OR FIB? 2

A CHALLENGING GAME OF TRUE OR FALSE

FACT
OR
FIB? 2

A CHALLENGING GAME
OF TRUE OR FALSE

KATHY FURGANG

STERLING CHILDREN'S BOOKS
New York

STERLING CHILDREN'S BOOKS
New York

An Imprint of Sterling Publishing
387 Park Avenue South
New York, NY 10016

ISBN 978-1-4549-0983-5
Design by M. Johnson
Art Direction by Jennifer Browning

Library of Congress Cataloging-in-Publication Data

Furgang, Kathy.
  Fact or fib? 2 : a challenging game of true or false / Kathy Furgang.
     pages cm
  ISBN 978-1-4549-0983-5
  1. Science--Miscellanea--Juvenile literature. 2. Scientific recreations--Juvenile literature. I. Title. II. Title: Fact or fib two.
  Q163.F872 2014
  500--dc23   2013024652

Distributed in Canada by Sterling Publishing
c/o Canadian Manda Group, 165 Dufferin Street
Toronto, Ontario, Canada M6K 3H6
Distributed in the United Kingdom by GMC Distribution Services
Castle Place, 166 High Street, Lewes, East Sussex, England BN7 1XU
Distributed in Australia by Capricorn Link (Australia) Pty. Ltd.
P.O. Box 704, Windsor, NSW 2756, Australia

For information about custom editions, special sales, and premium and corporate purchases,
please contact Sterling Special Sales at 800-805-5489 or specialsales@sterlingpublishing.com.
Manufactured in China

Lot #:
2 4 6 8 10 9 7 5 3 1
02/14

www.sterlingpublishing.com/kids

How much do you really know about the world around you? Can you tell a science fact from a science fib? **FACT** OR **FIB? 2** gives you tons of chances to test your knowledge of space, the human body, and technology. Here's how to play. The pages in this book are presented in sets of four. First, read the three statements on the pair of pages stamped **FACT OR FIB?** . Guess which two of these statements are totally true—and which one is a wacky whopper. Then turn the page to check your answers and get more interesting information about each statement.

Test your friends, your parents, or even your teacher! Then give them those little nuggets of knowledge that reveal the correct answer. They're sure to be surprised!

FACT OR FIB?

EACH HUMAN TONGUE PRINT IS UNIQUE.

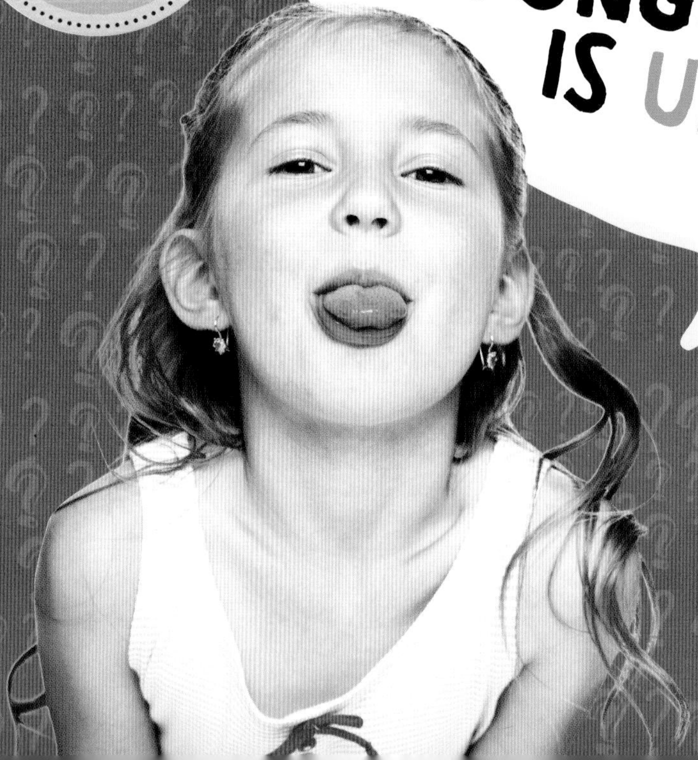

All **PLANETS** have moons.

The letters ".com" in a website address stand for commercial.

FACT

JUST LIKE FINGERPRINTS,
EVERY PERSON'S
TONGUE PRINT
IS THE ONLY ONE LIKE IT.
A TONGUE PRINT CAN HELP
IDENTIFY A PERSON.

FIB

MERCURY and VENUS have no moons. They are the two planets closest to the sun.

FACT

Web addresses that end in ".com" are used for businesses. Other sites may have ".org" for organization, ".gov" for government, or ".net" for network.

FACT OR FIB?

A comet's tail always travels behind it.

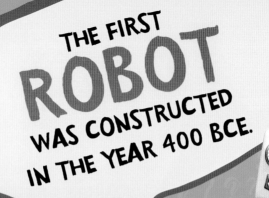

THE FIRST **ROBOT** WAS CONSTRUCTED IN THE YEAR 400 BCE.

The more you use your nails, the **faster** they will grow.

FIB

A comet's tail can be in front of the comet. The tail always moves away from the sun.

FACT THE GREEK MATHEMATICIAN

ARCHYTAS

IS SAID TO HAVE MADE THE VERY FIRST ROBOT. NAMED "THE PIGEON," THIS WOODEN BIRD WAS POWERED BY STEAM. AT ONE POINT IT FLEW AS FAR AS 200 METERS.

 FACT

Fingernails grow fastest on the longest fingers of the hand you write with. Your fingernails grow faster than your toenails because you use them more.

13

The length of
one year on Earth is
**365 DAYS, 5 HOURS,
48 MINUTES, AND
46 SECONDS.**

We blink less often
when using a computer.

PEOPLE ONLY GET GOOSE BUMPS WHEN THEY ARE COLD.

The "leftover" hours, minutes, and seconds every year add up to an extra day on our calendars about every four years. A year with an extra day is called a leap year.

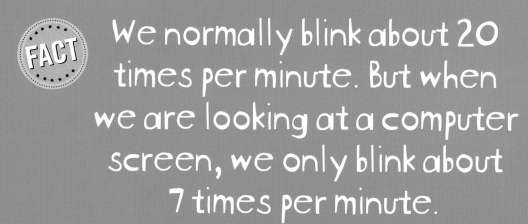

FACT We normally blink about 20 times per minute. But when we are looking at a computer screen, we only blink about 7 times per minute.

FIB

GOOSE BUMPS ALSO HAPPEN WHEN YOU ARE **SCARED, MAD, OR EXCITED.** THEY ARE THE BODY'S RESPONSE TO STRESS.

FACT OR FIB?

Remote controls began being sold with TVs in the **1950s**.

Humans shed about 600,000 tiny skin cells each hour.

PLUTO

WAS A PLANET FOR ONLY 76 YEARS.

It was not until the 1980s that televisions were sold with remote controls. Before that, you had to get up and turn a dial attached to the TV in order to change the channel.

You'll lose about 1.5 pounds (.68 kg) of skin cells per year, or 105 pounds (47.6 kg) by the time you are 70 years old. It's a good thing new skin cells are constantly taking the place of the ones that have been shed!

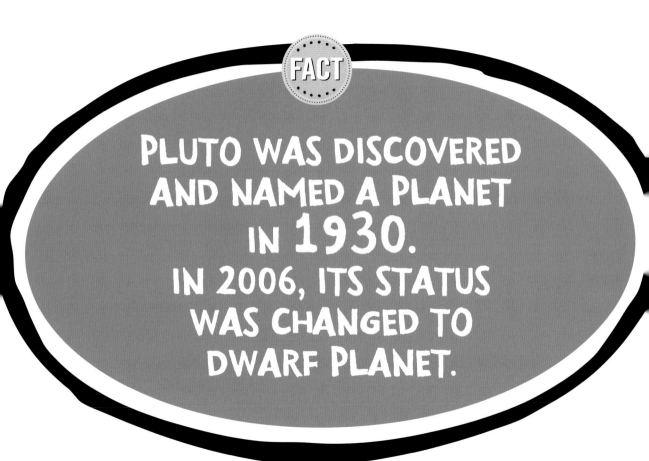

FACT

PLUTO WAS DISCOVERED AND NAMED A PLANET IN 1930.
IN 2006, ITS STATUS WAS CHANGED TO DWARF PLANET.

FACT OR FIB?

Your mouth has about **9,000** taste buds.

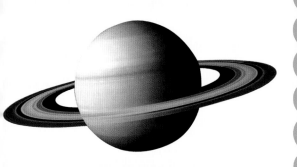

SATURN
is the only
PLANET
with
RINGS
around it.

COMPUTER CALCULATIONS ARE MEASURED IN UNITS CALLED **FLOPS**.

FACT

TASTE BUDS

are located on the tongue, throat, and roof of your mouth. They respond to the chemicals in food when they react with your saliva.

While Saturn is known for its rings made of ice, dust, and rock, it is not the only planet with rings. **JUPITER, URANUS,** and **NEPTUNE** also have rings around them.

A TERAFLOP IS A TRILLION CALCULATIONS PER SECOND. A PETAFLOP IS A QUADRILLION CALCULATIONS PER SECOND.

FACT

Your nose can remember **50,000** different scents.

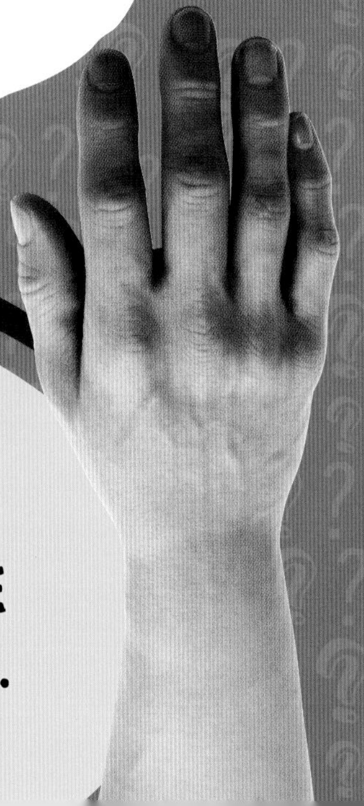

SOME MODERN ARTIFICIAL HANDS ARE CONTROLLED BY THE PATIENT'S OWN MUSCLES.

Mars is the HOTTEST planet.

It's hard to imagine there are even 50,000 different things to smell! What's more, dogs and other animals can remember a lot more scents than humans.

FACT

FACT

MUSCLES GIVE OFF SMALL ELECTRICAL SIGNALS WHEN THEY CONTRACT. THESE SIGNALS CAN BE USED TO CONTROL ARTIFICIAL BODY PARTS THAT ARE ATTACHED TO MUSCLES.

FIB

The hottest planet is Venus, where surface temperatures reach 864° Farenheit (462° C). The planet is surrounded by a very thick atmosphere that traps heat. It is so hot that soft metals like tin would melt on Venus.

FACT OR FIB?

ABOUT 21% OF EARTH'S ATMOSPHERE IS MADE OF OXYGEN.

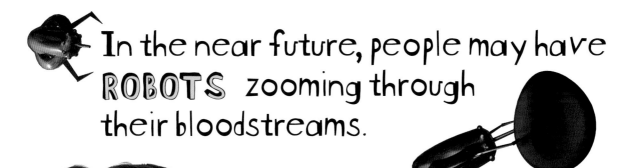

In the near future, people may have **ROBOTS** zooming through their bloodstreams.

A human sneeze can travel 50 miles (80 km) per hour.

THE ATMOSPHERE IS ALSO ABOUT 78% NITROGEN, 0.9% ARGON, 0.03% CARBON DIOXIDE, AND A SMALL AMOUNT OF OTHER ELEMENTS. WE GET MOST OF OUR OXYGEN FROM PLANTS.

FACT

NANOBOTS

are microscopic machines too small to be seen with your eyes. They will soon be used in medicine to fight cancer and other diseases.

FIB

A sneeze can actually travel faster than 100 miles (160 km) per hour. That's faster than a cheetah running at top speed!

FACT OR FIB?

All of the eight planets in our **SOLAR SYSTEM** orbit the sun in the same direction.

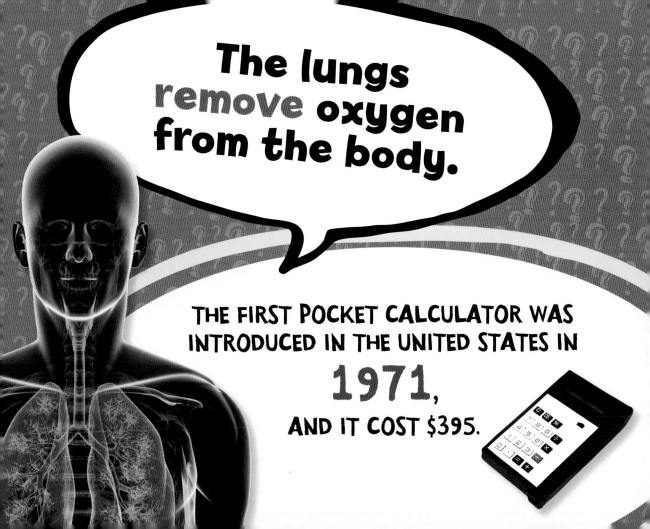

FACT

All eight planets move around the sun in a **COUNTERCLOCKWISE** direction. That is, if you are looking down on the planets from above.

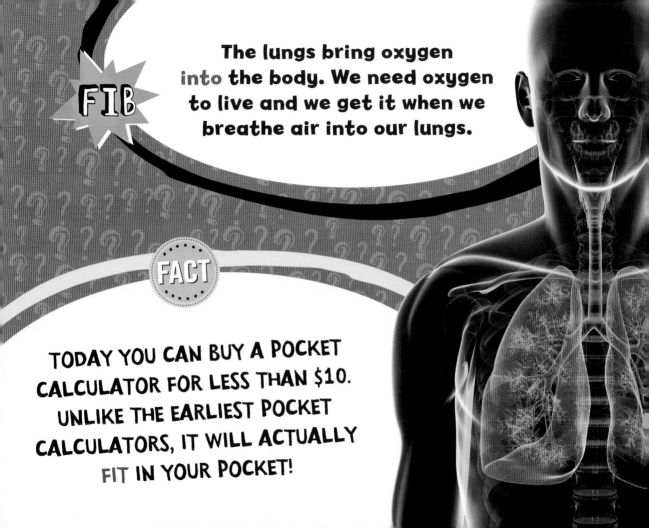

FIB

The lungs bring oxygen into the body. We need oxygen to live and we get it when we breathe air into our lungs.

FACT

TODAY YOU CAN BUY A POCKET CALCULATOR FOR LESS THAN $10. UNLIKE THE EARLIEST POCKET CALCULATORS, IT WILL ACTUALLY FIT IN YOUR POCKET!

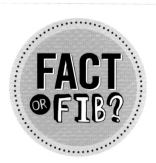

FACT OR **FIB?**

The computers that helped land man on the moon were **LESS** powerful than today's cell phones.

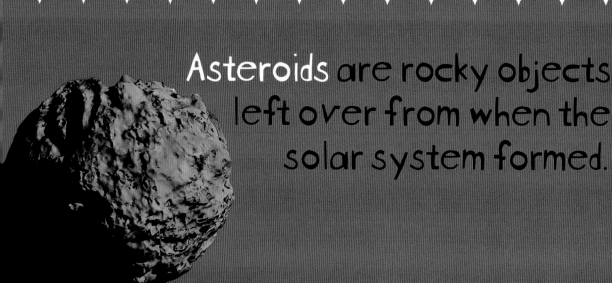

Asteroids are rocky objects left over from when the solar system formed.

SOME PEOPLE DON'T **DREAM** WHEN THEY SLEEP AT NIGHT.

APOLLO 11's computer system also had less memory than a modern cell phone. But there were hundreds of people hard at work to make the moon mission a success!

Asteroids have been floating around in space since the solar system was formed 4.6 billion years ago.

FACT

FIB

EVERYONE DREAMS DURING A NORMAL SLEEP CYCLE. THE PERIOD CALLED RAPID EYE MOVEMENT, OR REM, IS THE TIME WHEN PEOPLE DREAM VIVIDLY. HOWEVER, NOT EVERYONE REMEMBERS WHAT THEY DREAM!

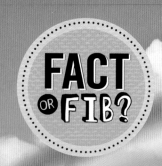

FACT
OR FIB?

There are **EIGHT**
colors in the rainbow.

THERE ARE 27 BONES IN THE HUMAN HAND AND WRIST.

It takes about TEN YEARS of higher education to become an astronomer.

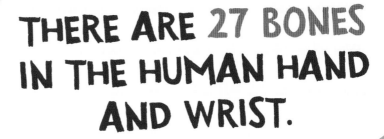

There are seven colors in the rainbow. They are: RED, ORANGE, YELLOW, GREEN, BLUE, INDIGO, and VIOLET. You can remember their names and order by remembering the name

ROY G. BIV.

Each letter stands for a color in the rainbow.

THERE ARE EIGHT BONES IN THE WRIST, TWO IN THE THUMB, AND THREE IN EACH OF THE OTHER FOUR FINGERS. THERE IS ALSO ONE BONE FOR EACH FINGER THAT CONNECTS THE PALM TO THE WRIST.

FACT

FACT

To become an astronomer, one must first spend four years earning a bachelor's degree. After that, graduate school takes about six years.

Venus can be seen
from Earth without a
TELESCOPE.

THERE ARE SIX BILLION ACTIVE CELL PHONES AROUND THE WORLD.

Everyone has the SAME number of eyelashes.

VENUS, MERCURY, MARS, JUPITER, and SATURN

can all be seen from Earth without a telescope. These planets are called classical planets. They can be seen at various times of the year.

FACT

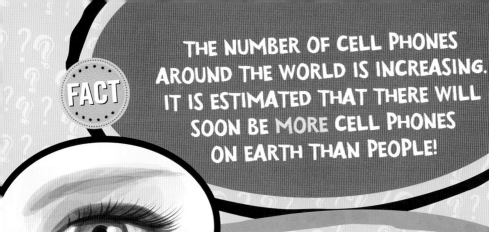

FACT

THE NUMBER OF CELL PHONES AROUND THE WORLD IS INCREASING. IT IS ESTIMATED THAT THERE WILL SOON BE MORE CELL PHONES ON EARTH THAN PEOPLE!

The number of eyelashes varies from person to person. There may be about 70 to 150 lashes on the upper eyelid and about 60 to 80 on the lower lid.

FIB

FACT OR FIB?

NEWBORN BABIES SLEEP ABOUT 16 HOURS PER DAY.

The world's fastest computer can perform nearly **17 quadrillion calculations per second.**

Earth is the center of the universe.

FACT NEWBORNS SLEEP FOR THE MAJORITY OF EACH DAY. HOWEVER, MOST ONLY SLEEP FOR ABOUT TWO TO FOUR HOURS AT A TIME.

FACT

The supercomputer, called the Titan, is in a computer laboratory in California. In the future, there will likely be an even faster computer.

FIB

For thousands of years, people believed that Earth was the center of the universe. But astronomers finally proved that the center of the solar system is actually the Sun.

Astronauts are taller when they are in space.

THE SUN IS ABOUT **100 BILLION** YEARS OLD.

Eating spinach can help improve your **MEMORY**.

FACT

In space, there is no gravity pulling down on the body. This stretches the spine, making it longer than it is on Earth.

FACT

Spinach has **FOLATE** and vitamins **K** and **E**. These vitamins can help you remember things. Broccoli, brussels sprouts, and cabbage can help improve your memory too.

Earth's upper atmosphere is filled with millions of pieces of debris, called **SPACE JUNK**. Discarded satellites, the remnants of spacecraft explosions, and broken rocket pieces are all just floating up in space.

FIB

THE AVERAGE HEAD OF HAIR IS MADE OF ABOUT 100,000 STRANDS. BLONDES HAVE AN AVERAGE OF ABOUT 140,000 HAIRS. REDHEADS HAVE ABOUT 90,000 HAIRS.

FACT

Cirrus clouds

are thin, wispy clouds over 18,000 feet (about 5.5 km) in the air. They are made mostly of ice crystals.

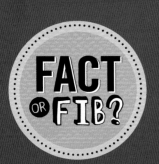

FACT OR FIB?

Our noses help us taste

FOOD.

Uranus has more than 27 MOONS.

STRAWBERRIES, BLUEBERRIES, AND RASPBERRIES ARE ALL THE SAME TYPE OF FRUIT.

FACT

Taste buds in our mouths recognize sweet, sour, bitter, and salty. Our noses receive the smell of the food and send SIGNALS to the brain. Together, our noses and mouths help us taste.

Uranus has many very small moons. Some are so

SMALL

they are confused with asteroids. The exact number is not known, but there are at least 27.

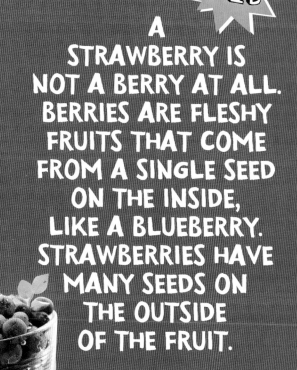

FIB

A STRAWBERRY IS NOT A BERRY AT ALL. BERRIES ARE FLESHY FRUITS THAT COME FROM A SINGLE SEED ON THE INSIDE, LIKE A BLUEBERRY. STRAWBERRIES HAVE MANY SEEDS ON THE OUTSIDE OF THE FRUIT.

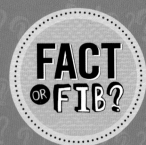

FACT OR FIB?

The human appendix is an important part of the digestive system.

FIB

Humans no longer use the appendix. Though scientists are not certain of the function of the appendix, it can be removed with no harmful effects.

A SPACE SUIT HAS 13 LAYERS OF MATERIAL AND MUST KEEP THE ASTRONAUT ALIVE IN SPACE. THE SUIT CONTROLS TEMPERATURE, AIR PRESSURE, AND PROVIDES OXYGEN TO THE ASTRONAUT WHO WEARS IT.

FACT

FACT

The first mouse was made in **1964** out of wood. It had two gears as wheels and one button on the top.

Smelly feet are caused by sweat.

Computer programming is one of the fastest growing careers.

THE WEATHER AROUND YOU COULD BE DIFFERENT IF YOU GO JUST A MILE IN ANY DIRECTION. CHANGING WEATHER IS CAUSED BY A MIX OF DIFFERENT TEMPERATURES AND AIR PRESSURES MEETING EACH OTHER.

FACT

People have about 500,000 sweat glands between their two feet, and can make a pint (.47 L) of sweat every day.

 FACT

Computers are becoming more and more important to daily life. To create new and improved programs in the future, there will be a greater need for **computer programmers.**

FACT
OR FIB?

It is **NOT** possible for you to tickle yourself.

There is no
WIND
on the
MOON.

THERE ARE MORE TRADITIONAL PHONES THAN CELL PHONES IN THE WORLD.

FACT

You cannot respond to a tickle from **YOURSELF** in the same way that you would respond to a tickle from someone else. That's because your brain knows how your fingers will be moving, where, and for how long.

During the
first moon landing
in **1969**,
astronauts left
footprints in the dirt.
They are still there
today because there
is **NO WIND**
to blow them away.

THERE ARE MORE
CELL PHONES
IN THE WORLD
THAN LAND LINES.
MORE THAN
ONE THOUSAND
MOBILE PHONES
ARE ACTIVATED
EVERY MINUTE.

FIB

FACT OR FIB?

POLICE CAN MORE EASILY TRACK AND CATCH CRIMINALS WHO USE SMART PHONES.

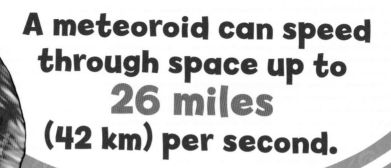

A meteoroid can speed through space up to **26 miles** (42 km) per second.

The PENCILS you write with in school are made of lead.

FACT

MANY SMART PHONES HAVE A GLOBAL-POSITIONING SYSTEM, OR GPS. DETECTIVES CAN USE IT TO TRACK THE MOVEMENTS OF CRIMINALS.

FACT

Meteoroids travel so fast because space has no air or winds to slow down moving objects.

FIB

Although they are called lead pencils, there is no lead in pencils. Pencils are made of GRAPHITE surrounded by wood.

81

NINETY PERCENT of robots work in factories.

When you lose weight, you lose fat cells.

FACT

Many factory jobs are **AUTOMATED**, or done by machines. Factories that make cars are the most automated of all. In auto factories, most jobs are being done robotically.

Fat cells can shrink, but not disappear completely. Your fat cells are with you forever.

FIB

FACT

YOUR CHANCES OF BEING STRUCK BY A METEOR FROM SPACE ARE EXTREMELY LOW. MOST METEORS THAT STRIKE EARTH LAND IN OCEANS, SINCE THEY COVER OVER 70% OF THE PLANET'S SURFACE.

FACT OR FIB?

SCIENTIST NIKOLA TESLA WAS A FAMOUS ASTRONOMER.

The sun will shine for at least another 7 BILLION YEARS.

Broken bones **heal** faster the younger you are.

FIB

TESLA
IS KNOWN FOR HIS WORK AND CONTRIBUTIONS TO THE STUDY OF ELECTRICITY.

The sun is not even halfway through its expected life cycle. It has been around for over **4.5 BILLION YEARS**, and scientists think it has another 7 billion years to go.

A young child's broken bone may take as little as three weeks to heal. A teen's or adult's may take six to ten weeks to heal.

89

FACT OR FIB?

During an 8-hour period, a robotic arm can pick up and arrange 2,000 chocolates into boxed assortments.

FIB

A robot in a chocolate factory can actually sort about 20,000 chocolates in a workday!

HYPEROPIA IS ANOTHER WORD FOR

FARSIGHTEDNESS.

IT IS A COMMON VISION PROBLEM IN WHICH A PERSON CANNOT SEE OBJECTS THAT ARE CLOSE.

If you measured around the middle, Earth is about 24,854 miles (40,000 km). And the sun is more than 2,713,406 miles (4,379,000 km) around the middle. The sun is a lot BIGGER than any of the planets.

An apple will **FLOAT** in water.

The first handheld mobile phone was made in 1973.

HEAD LICE SPREADS BY **FLYING** FROM PERSON TO PERSON.

An apple will float because it is **25% air**.
This makes it lighter than water and allows it to float.

The company **Motorola** made the first mobile phone, which was not sold to the public for another 11 years. And when it did go on sale in 1984, it cost nearly $4,000!

FACT

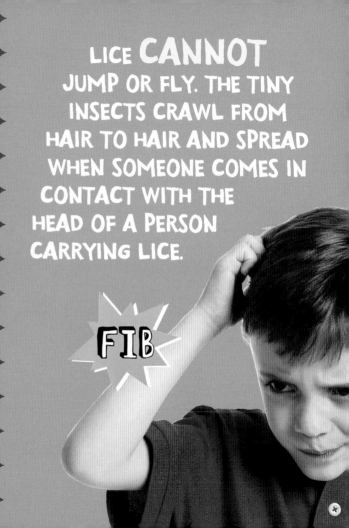

LICE **CANNOT** JUMP OR FLY. THE TINY INSECTS CRAWL FROM HAIR TO HAIR AND SPREAD WHEN SOMEONE COMES IN CONTACT WITH THE HEAD OF A PERSON CARRYING LICE.

FIB

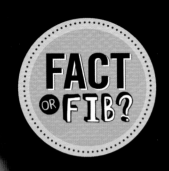

In the future, the sun will get so large it will reach Mercury, Venus, and possibly Earth.

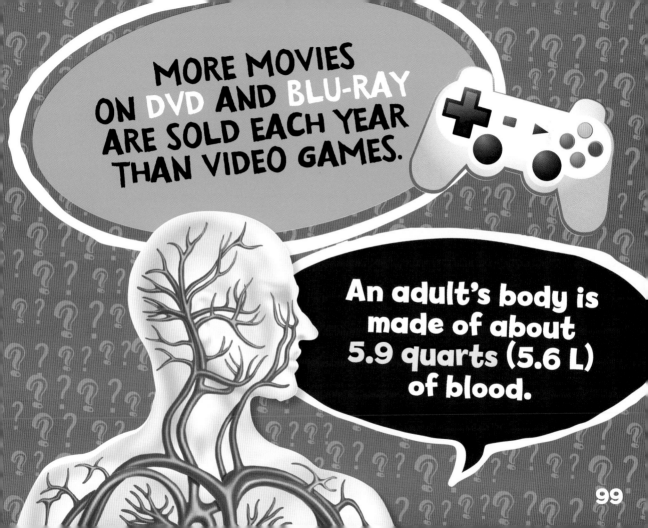

In billions of years, the sun will become a red giant, which means that it will grow to many times its current size. Look out, planets!

VIDEO GAMES ARE SO POPULAR
THAT THEY HAVE BEEN OUTSELLING
MOVIES SINCE 2008.

FIB

FACT

The blood plays an important
part in delivering oxygen and
nutrients to our cells. It also
helps to get rid of waste.

101

FACT OR FIB?

All of the fish that are caught are sold as food.

The car was the FIRST product to be made on a moving assembly line.

102

A BLACK HOLE
IS WHAT HAPPENS
WHEN A HUGE STAR
COLLAPSES ONTO ITSELF.

FIB **About 25% of the fish that are caught are used to make products, such as glue, soap, and fertilizer.**

FACT

Henry Ford invented the moving assembly line with conveyor belts. It was used in his Michigan factory around 1913 to build the Ford Model T car. The process eventually allowed the factory to produce a car every 93 minutes.

FACT

A BLACK HOLE OCCURS WHEN A STAR IS DYING. AN EXPLODING STAR IS CALLED A SUPERNOVA.

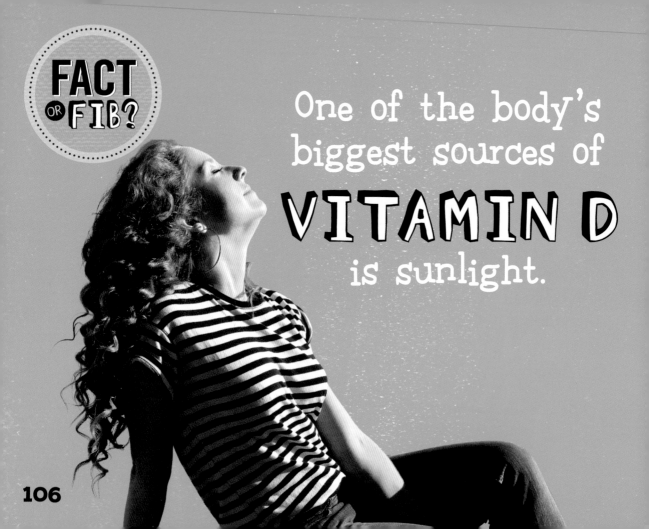

FACT OR FIB?

One of the body's biggest sources of **VITAMIN D** is sunlight.

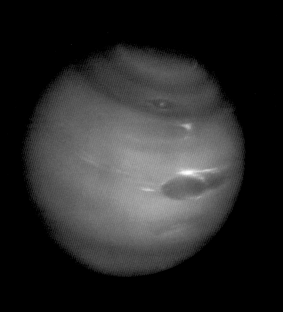

The length of a year is the same on **NEPTUNE** as it is on Earth.

PEANUTS ARE USED TO MAKE DYNAMITE.

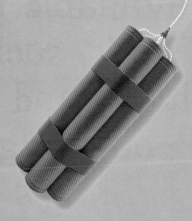

FACT Our bodies MAKE vitamin D when sunlight hits our skin. It is also available naturally in some foods, such as meats, eggs, cheese, and milk. This vitamin helps fight diseases and keeps bones strong.

FIB

A **YEAR** is the amount of time it takes a planet to orbit the sun. It takes Neptune 165 Earth years to orbit the sun!

GLYCEROL IS ONE OF THE INGREDIENTS USED IN DYNAMITE. IT IS MADE FROM **PEANUT OIL!**

FACT

HUMANS HAVE NOT STEPPED FOOT ON ANY PLANET OTHER THAN EARTH.

The first stay-on tab for soda cans was invented in **1974.**

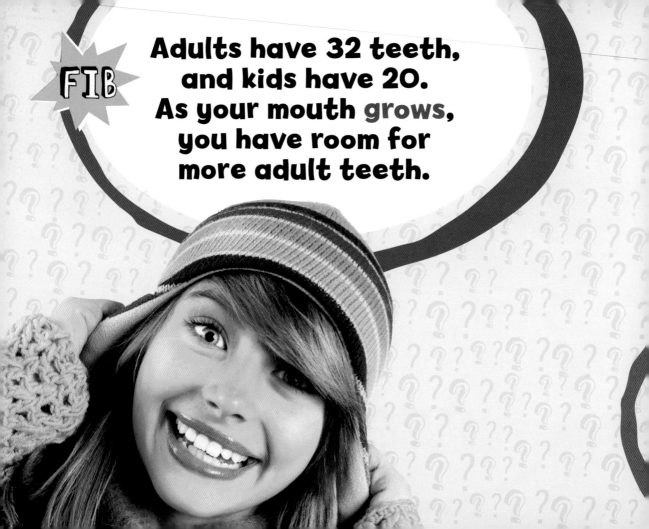

 **FACT** HUMANS HAVE WALKED ON THE MOON, BUT ASTRONAUTS HAVE NOT WALKED ON OTHER PLANETS. HOWEVER, ROBOTS AND PROBES HAVE BEEN SENT TO EXPLORE OTHER PLANETS, SUCH AS MARS.

The **STAY-ON** soda tab cut down on litter. People no longer had to get rid of a tab when they opened a can of soda.  **FACT**

The **SMALLEST** bone in your body is in your ear.

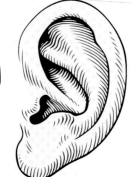

One liter of drinking water contains about **100,000** bacteria.

FACT

The stirrup is a tiny bone in the middle ear. It is only .11 inches (2.8 mm) long.

Luckily, most of the bacteria in drinking water is HARMLESS to the human body.

FACT

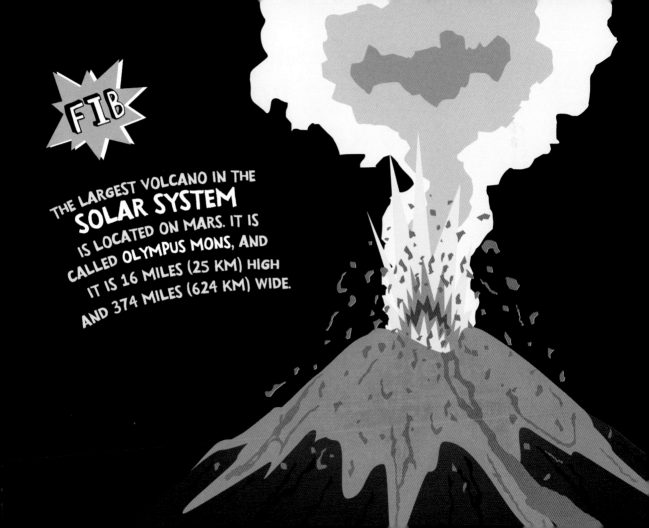

FIB

THE LARGEST VOLCANO IN THE **SOLAR SYSTEM** IS LOCATED ON MARS. IT IS CALLED OLYMPUS MONS, AND IT IS 16 MILES (25 KM) HIGH AND 374 MILES (624 KM) WIDE.

EACH AMERICAN EATS ABOUT **22 POUNDS** (ABOUT 10 KG) OF TOMATOES EVERY YEAR.

The can opener was **INVENTED** a year after the invention of the tin can.

MORE THAN HALF OF THE TOTAL AMOUNT OF TOMATOES AMERICANS EAT IS IN THE FORM OF **TOMATO SAUCE OR KETCHUP.**

FACT

The can opener was not invented until **48 YEARS** after the tin can! The first tin cans were too thick for a can opener to cut through them.

FIB

Sound needs air to travel.
Since space has no air, sound cannot be heard.

FACT OR **FIB?**

ASTRONAUTS
train for hundreds
of hours before
going into space.

THE **LEFT SIDE** OF YOUR BRAIN MAKES THE LEFT SIDE OF YOUR BODY MOVE.

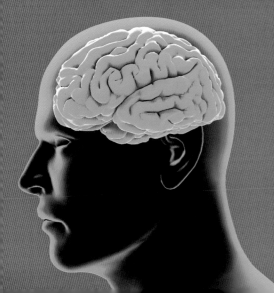

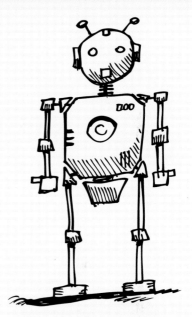

ROBOTS STOP

oil spills under the ocean.

FACT

An astronaut's training takes up to TWO YEARS. They have to learn to use a lot of equipment. And they need to know how to handle all types of different situations that may occur on their missions.

THE HUMAN BRAIN IS **BALANCED** IN SUCH A WAY THAT THE LEFT SIDE OF THE BRAIN CONTROLS THE RIGHT SIDE OF THE BODY. AND YOU GUESSED IT! THE RIGHT SIDE OF THE BRAIN CONTROLS THE LEFT SIDE OF THE BODY.

FIB

FACT

THERE ARE ROBOTS WORKING **DEEP** UNDER THE SEA WHERE OIL IS DRILLED. HUMANS OPERATE THEM TO CHECK FOR AND STOP OIL SPILLS.

Astronauts on the **INTERNATIONAL SPACE STATION** can choose from a menu of more than 100 foods.

Washington State grows about 60% of the apples that are eaten in the United States.

Astronauts in space eat **THREE MEALS** per day, plus snacks. The space station gets new food deliveries every few months.

Washington State makes a lot of apples, especially Red Delicious, Golden Delicious, Granny Smith, and Gala.

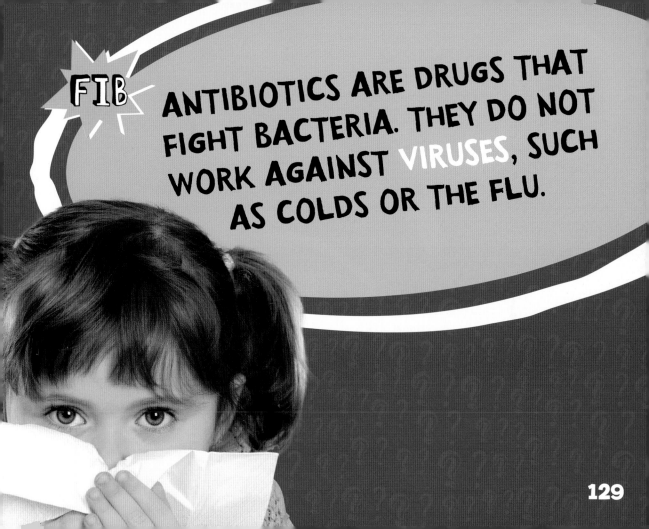

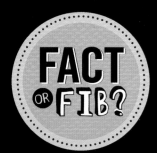

Astronauts in space can **receive** email messages every day.

FACT

Email **helps** astronauts to not feel bored or lonely. In addition to daily emails, they can receive weekly video calls from home.

FIB

Your heart actually beats about **100,000** times a day! That's over a billion heartbeats by your 30th birthday.

FACT

EINSTEIN
WAS ONE OF THE WORLD'S MOST FAMOUS SCIENTISTS. HE ENCOURAGED CURIOSITY. HE SAID, "FOR KNOWLEDGE IS LIMITED, WHEREAS IMAGINATION EMBRACES THE ENTIRE WORLD."

FACT OR FIB?

Compared to the other planets in the solar system, **URANUS** is lying on its side.

The average child aged eight to 18 spends seven and a half hours a day using some form of technology.

Instead of spinning from left to right like Earth, Uranus spins from TOP to BOTTOM.

Children use technology in the form of computers, video games, cell phones, and computers.

UP TO EIGHT OUT OF EVERY TEN PEOPLE CAN ROLL THEIR TONGUE. SCIENTISTS SAY THE ABILITY IS PARTLY PASSED DOWN FROM PARENT TO CHILD. SOME CHILDREN MAY LEARN THE TRICK OVER TIME.

FIB

FACT OR FIB?

OVHD

STS-120
ISS 10A

Astronauts must be tied to the floor, wall, or ceiling when they sleep in space.

Light enters your eye through the iris.

SOME E-BOOK READERS OR TABLETS CAN HOLD MORE BOOKS THAN A SMALL LIBRARY.

FACT

There is a lot less gravity in space than there is on Earth. Astronauts could float away during sleep unless they are held in place.

The iris is the colored part of your eye. Light enters your eye through the pupil, which is the dark circle in the center of your eye.

SOME HANDHELD ELECTRONIC READERS CAN HOLD UP TO 6,000 BOOKS.

Life has been found on **MARS**.

The traffic light and the gas mask were invented by the same person.

142

SOME MESSAGES
TRAVEL TO AND FROM
THE BRAIN AT UP TO
170 MILES (274 KM)
PER HOUR.

Life has not been found on Mars or any other planet in our solar system. However, scientists do think there may have once been tiny bacteria-like life forms on Mars.

FIB

Inventor and businessman Garrett Morgan was the son of former slaves. He invented the gas mask in 1914 and the traffic light in 1923.

FACT

FACT

THE FASTEST BRAIN SIGNALS ARE CALLED NERVE IMPULSES THEY TRAVEL VERY FAST THROUGH THE BODY. THAT'S WHY YOU CAN REACT SO QUICKLY WHEN YOU BURN YOUR HAND OR STUB YOUR TOE.

Our galaxy is called the MILKY WAY.

The galaxy is shaped like a giant, rotating WHIRLPOOL. Our solar system is located in one of the branches, or trails, of the galaxy's large spiraling shape.

FACT

Bell went on to invent other things, but the telephone was his most famous invention.

FIB

THE BRAIN IS THE BODY PART THAT USES THE MOST OXYGEN. IT USES ABOUT 20% OF THE OXYGEN YOU BREATHE IN. AND YET IT ONLY TAKES UP ABOUT 2% OF YOUR BODY'S MASS.

FACT
OR FIB?

It takes light
100,000
years to cross from one
side of the galaxy
to the other.

Most
DREAMS
are about
TEN
minutes long.

AN
OBJECT THAT
IS AS LONG AS A
NANOMETER
IS TOO SMALL
TO SEE WITH
JUST OUR
EYES.

The galaxy is so large that it contains at least **100 BILLION STARS** It takes 200 million years for it to rotate.

FACT

Most
of our dreams are
no longer than
two
or
three
seconds. And we
don't even remember
most of them.

FIB

FACT

A
NANOMETER
IS A
TINY UNIT OF
MEASUREMENT.
THERE ARE
25,400,000
NANOMETERS
IN JUST ONE INCH
(2.5 CM).

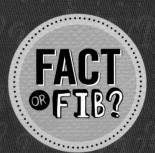

FACT OR FIB?

Facial hair is the **fastest** growing hair on the human body.

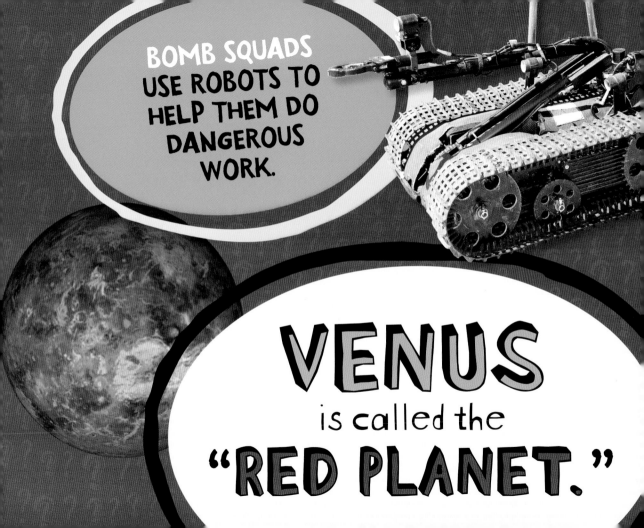

FACT

If a man never shaved during his whole lifetime, his beard would be more than **30 feet (9 m) long.**

A MOBILE, CRUISING ROBOT THAT LOOKS LIKE A MINI ARMORED TANK ROLLS INTO DANGEROUS PLACES. IT CAN EVEN CLIMB STAIRS TO LOCATE AND GET RID OF BOMBS.

MARS

is the planet called the "Red Planet" because of its orange-red appearance. The color occurs because of rust in the planet's rocky surface.

Spacecrafts are made on **ASSEMBLY LINES** like cars.

A BANANA WITH BROWN SPOTS TASTES SWEETER THAN ONE THAT IS ALL YELLOW.

158

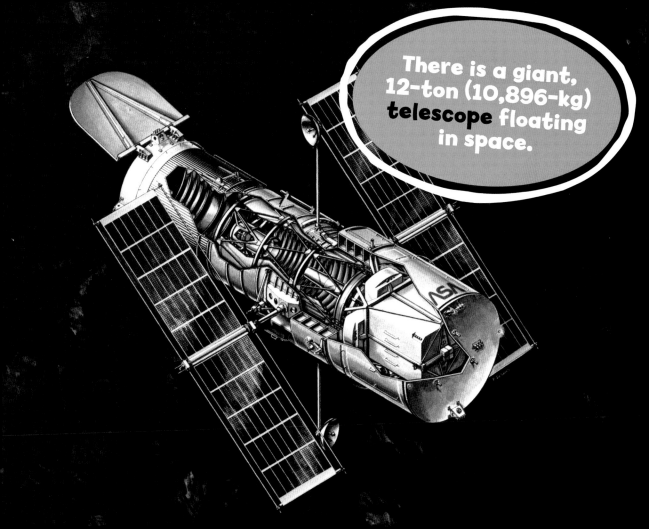

Most spacecrafts are **CUSTOM** made to do a special job. Each is designed and built in a special way.

FIB

FACT

THE **STARCH** IN BANANAS TURNS TO SUGAR AS THE FRUIT RIPENS AND GETS BROWN SPOTS. BROWNISH BANANAS MAY NOT LOOK AS NICE AS YELLOW ONES WITHOUT SPOTS, BUT THEY HAVE A SWEETER TASTE.

FACT

The
Hubble Space Telescope
is 43 feet (13 m) long.
It takes amazing photos of
space for scientists
to study.

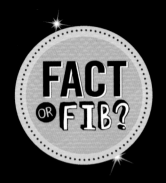

FACT OR **FIB?**

In ancient times, people were afraid when they saw

COMETS

in the sky.

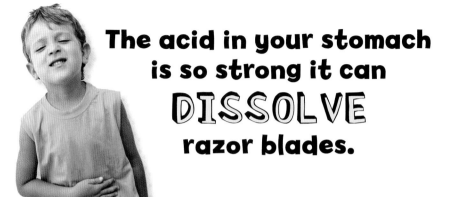

The acid in your stomach is so strong it can **DISSOLVE** razor blades.

EACH YEAR, MORE AND MORE PEOPLE ARE USING VIDEO CAMERAS.

Before scientists understood that comets were just balls of rock and ice, people were scared of them. They thought that comets were **BAD LUCK**.

FACT The HYDROCHLORIC ACID in your stomach is very strong. It can dissolve any type of food, as well as many types of metals.

FIB THE NUMBER OF VIDEO CAMERAS IS DECREASING. MORE AND MORE PEOPLE ARE USING THEIR SMART PHONES TO RECORD EVENTS.

THE AVERAGE PERSON PASSES GAS ABOUT 14 TIMES PER DAY.

The POPSICLE was invented by an 11-year-old.

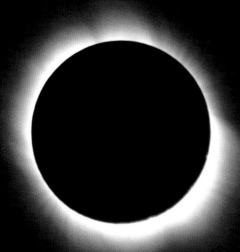

In a solar eclipse, the sun passes in front of the moon.

THE PROCESS OF DIGESTION PRODUCES GASES THAT MUST BE RELEASED FROM THE BODY. THEY WOULD BE PAINFUL AND HARMFUL IF THEY WERE TRAPPED IN THE ABDOMEN AND NOT RELEASED.

In 1905, a boy left his drink with a mixing stick outside on a cold night and it froze. This gave him the idea for the frozen treat.

FIB

A solar eclipse happens when the moon passes in front of the sun and **covers** its light.

FACT OR FIB?

BEFORE WRIST WATCHES, PEOPLE USED TO CARRY THEIR WATCHES IN THEIR POCKETS.

EAR WAX is a sign of poor hygiene.

A compass will not work on the moon.

POCKET WATCHES
WERE POPULAR FROM THE LATE 1600s
TO THE LATE 1800s. WHEN WRIST WATCHES
FIRST BECAME AVAILABLE IN THE 1800s,
THEY WERE DESIGNED FOR

WOMEN

FACT

TO WEAR.

Ear wax is a sign of GOOD EAR HEALTH. It is produced to protect your ear from bacteria, fungus, and even insects and dirt. It is a natural cleanser for your ear canal.

FACT

The moon does not have a magnetic field. So, unlike on Earth, a compass needle cannot point north.

173

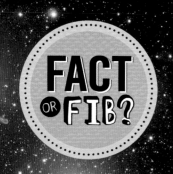

FACT OR FIB?

Red stars are **HOTTER** than blue stars.

Every day,
there are about
300 MILLION
photos uploaded
to **FACEBOOK.**

THERE IS
WATER
INSIDE EACH
KERNEL OF
POPCORN.

FIB

Red stars are the
COOLEST,
at about
4,500° Fahrenheit (2,500° C).
Blue stars are the
HOTTEST
and can reach up to
72,000° F (40,000° C).

Facebook has many users. The 300 million photos **UPLOADED** each day translates to about one picture uploaded by each member every three days.

WHEN A POPCORN KERNEL HEATS UP, THE WATER INSIDE EXPANDS. THIS MAKES THE KERNEL EXPLODE. THE SOFT STARCH INSIDE THEN GROWS UP TO **50%** ITS ORIGINAL SIZE.

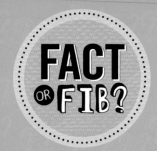
FACT OR FIB?

Students started wearing **HEADPHONES** in the classroom when computers in school became popular.

The first object to be seen through a microscope was a sliver of cork.

The average person produces enough saliva in a lifetime to fill two swimming pools.

Before the computer, students had been using headphones in school since the 1950s. They used them to listen to **AUDIO TAPES**, which is still done in many classrooms today.

FIB

In 1665, English scientist Robert Hooke looked at a cork through a microscope and described what he called small "cells" or "pores." He was the first to use the word "cell" to describe these tiny structures.

FACT

FACT

Saliva is the first step in your digestion process. It helps to break down foods and it keeps your mouth from getting too dry.

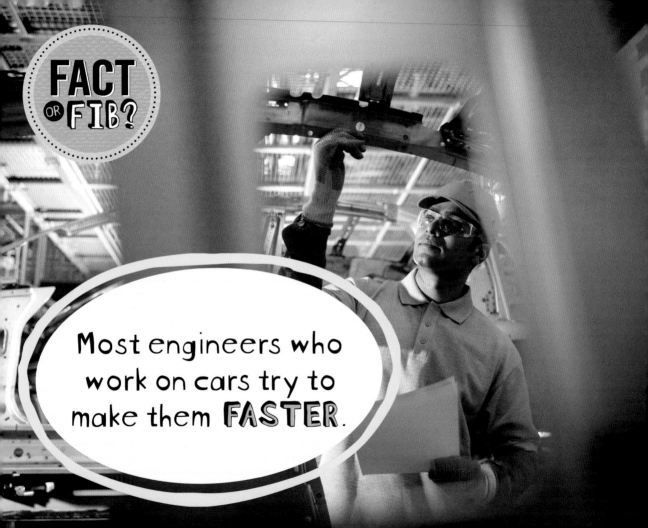

FIB

Most car engineers work to

MAKE CARS SAFER.

They perform tests and build car parts to keep people from getting hurt in a crash.

About one in 2,000 newborns have a tooth that has already broken through the gums.

SOME APPS WORK WITH A SENSOR THAT YOU PLACE ON YOUR FINGER. THE SENSOR HELPS GET IMPORTANT INFORMATION ABOUT YOUR BODY AND HEALTH.

FACT
OR FIB?

Scientists can tell
EXACTLY
where raindrops
are in the sky.

When an astronaut
returns to Earth,
it is hard to walk
and lift objects.

ABOUT 10% OF PEOPLE HAVE NO SENSE OF SMELL.

Scientists use a weather technology in which **RADIO WAVES** bounce off objects in the air, such as rain or snow. It is called **DOPPLER RADAR**. This lets scientists know the exact location of anything the radio waves hit.

FACT

FACT

An astronaut's body adjusts to life in a weightless environment. This causes muscles and bones to weaken. When the astronaut returns to Earth's gravity, the chance of breaking a bone is much greater.

FIB

ONLY ABOUT 2% OF THE POPULATION DOESN'T HAVE A WORKING SENSE OF SMELL. THE INABILITY TO SMELL IS CALLED **ANOSMIA**.

A person could not live for more than three days without food.

THERE IS MORE **PROTEIN** IN A CUP OF MILK THAN IN AN EGG.

MILK

FACT

Much of the ocean is the deep sea, where humans have trouble reaching. Recently, scientists have set up seafloor observatories to examine life at the bottom of the ocean.

As long as drinkable water is available, a person can live for a month or two without food. The more body fat a person started with, the longer he or she would survive.

FIB

FACT

A CUP OF MILK HAS **8 GRAMS** OF PROTEIN. AN EGG HAS ONLY 6 GRAMS OF PROTEIN.

The first artificial limbs were made over

300

years ago.

It takes several kinds of **ROBOTS** and **BIG MACHINES** to make a can of mixed nuts.

A PERSON SUFFERING FROM LACK OF SLEEP CAN SEE THINGS THAT ARE NOT THERE.

An artificial limb
was found on a

3,000-

year-old mummy
in ancient Egypt.

FIB

The mixed nuts you buy in a store have been **SHELLED** by machines. A different machine is used for each type of nut. They are then sorted by robots.

FACT

AFTER DAYS OF NO SLEEP, A PERSON CAN THINK THEY'RE SEEING THINGS THAT AREN'T THERE. THESE ARE CALLED HALLUCINATIONS. THIS ODD EXPERIENCE STOPS WHEN THE PERSON GETS SOME SLEEP.

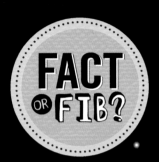

FACT OR **FIB?**

NOTHING CAN ESCAPE FROM A BLACK HOLE IN SPACE.

Thomas Jefferson invented a special kind of eyeglasses.

It takes more muscles to frown than it does to smile.

THE PULL OF GRAVITY IS SO STRONG INSIDE A BLACK HOLE THAT EVEN LIGHT CANNOT ESCAPE.

FACT

Benjamin Franklin invented bifocal eyeglasses. These special glasses are made of two lenses in one frame— one for seeing far away, and one for seeing up close.

FIB

There are 43 muscles in the face that are needed to form a frown. Only 17 muscles are used to form a smile.

FACT

INDEX

NOTE: Page numbers in parentheses indicate FACT or FIB answers.

A

Acid, in stomach, 163 (165)
Anosmia, 189
Antibiotics, 127 (129)
Appendix, 68 (70)
Apples, 94 (96), 126 (128)
Apps, smart phone, 183 (185)
Archytas, 13
Artificial body parts, 26 (28), 194 (196)
Assembly lines, 102 (104), 158 (160)
Asteroids, 38 (40)
Astronauts, 54 (56), 67 (69), 122 (124), 130 (132), 138 (140). See also Space
Astronomers, 43 (45), 53, 86 (88)

Atmosphere, 30 (32), 60

B

Babies, 50 (52), 183 (185)
Bacteria, 114 (116), 129, 144, 173
Bananas, 158 (160)
Bell, Alexander Graham, 149 (151)
Berries, 63 (65)
Black holes, 103 (105), 198 (200)
Blink rate, 14 (16)
Blood and bloodstream, 31 (33), 99 (101)
Bones, 43 (45), 87 (89), 108, 114 (116), 188
Books, e-book readers and, 139 (141)
Brain function, 76, 123 (125), 143 (145), 149

C

Calculators, pocket, 35 (37)
Can openers, 118 (120)
Car production, 182 (184)
Cars, 102 (104)
Cell/smart phones, 38 (40), 47 (49), 75 (77), 78 (80), 95 (97), 136, 165, 183 (185)
Children, technology and, 134 (136)
Clouds, 59 (61)
Colors, in rainbow, 42 (44)
Comets, 10 (12), 162 (164)
".com" meaning, 7 (9)
Compasses, 171 (173)
Computers
    calculation rate measurements, 23 (25)
    children on, 134 (136)
    eye blink rate and, 14 (16)
    fastest, 51 (53)

We hope you enjoyed all the fun facts (and fibs!) about space, the human body, and technology. Check out **FACT** OR **FIB?** if you want to test your knowledge of dinosaurs, bugs, and animals!